HOLDING SPACE SERIES
OIL IN YOUR GIFTING
E. Claudette Freeman, Convener and Editor

I0152760

©November 2021 by Zora James Publishing
An Imprint of Pecan Tree Publishing
Hollywood, FL 33020
www.zorajamespublishing.com
www.pecantreebooks.com

Scripture quotations are from those listed here.

THE AUTHORIZED (KING JAMES) VERSION. Rights in the Authorized Version in the United Kingdom are vested in the Crown. Reproduced by permission of the Crown's patentee, Cambridge University Press.

THE AMPLIFIED BIBLE, Old Testament copyright © 1965, 1987 by the Zondervan Corporation. The Amplified New Testament copyright © 1958, 1987 by The Lockman Foundation. Used by permission.

THE HOLY BIBLE, NEW INTERNATIONAL VERSION °. Copyright © 1973, 1978, 1984 by International Bible Society. Used by permission of Zondervan Publishing House. All rights reserved.

THE HOLY BIBLE, NEW LIVING TRANSLATION, copyright © 1996, 2004, 2007 by Tyndale House Foundation. Used by permission of Tyndale House Publishers, Inc., Carol Stream, Illinois 60188. All rights reserved.

978-1-7372621-9-0 Paperback
978-1-7358295-9-3 E-Book

Library of Congress Control Number: 2021950116

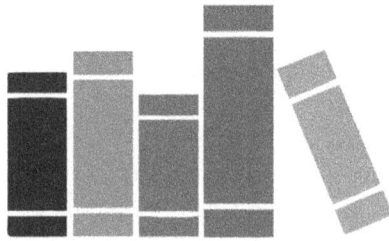

Zora James Publishing

Creating culturally and spiritually necessary
anthologies and collections.

A Pecan Tree Publishing Imprint
www.zorajamespublishing.com
Hollywood, FL

Contents

Oil in Your Gifting

Prayers and Devotionals for Creative Artists

E. CLAUDETTE FREEMAN, EDITOR

Introduction

The *Holding Space Series* is designed to offer prayers, affirmations, prophetic insight, and wisdom for those working in an array of categories and fields. Book one in the series *Oil in Your Gifting* which is now in your hands, was conceptualized for those in the vast arena of creative arts.

From vocalists to authors to fashion and interior designers; from musicians to poets and sculptors to culinary artists and every creative field in between - prayers and DEVOTIONALs in this edition of the series cover the gifting, talents and anointing of those called to the gift of creation.

The end of the work gives space for your interaction, affording space to write your vision and mission for the power in the work of your hands. Go forth, create, and minister through your art. May God be pleased.

E. Claudette Freeman

Opening Declaration

E. Claudette Freeman

Someone is awaiting your creation! Min. Chantaye Watson, randomly pops up and says to me, "Someone is counting on your stay." She shoots a text, mentions me in a social media post, gives me an unexpected phone call. "Claudie," she almost sings in her shortened version of my name, "Girl, someone is counting on your stay. I know it gets hard. I know it does. But stay the course. Your stay encourages me and others."

How often that reminder of hers comes at a moment I am telling God, I am really giving up. No, FOR REAL this time I'm done.

I heard my sweet Chantaye's voice, as I sat the VIVA Women's Conference, hosted by Potential Church in Cooper City, Florida. Conference speaker, Pastor Kim "Real Talk Kim" Jones spoke a sentence during her sermon that knocked me off my seat. She said, "Someone is waiting on your transformation to get them to theirs."

Shut ALL THE DOORS! Guess I wasn't giving up or giving in – again!

We have an assignment to fulfill in the Earth. Even when the bullies abound in our schoolyard (our life). Even when the purpose we know we are called to live out has us looking like the biggest fool ever to everyone around us. Even when the fight has us bloodied and bruised. There is something about an anointed creative that won't allow us to lay down and throw away the tools of our trade. Instead, the anointed creative hears a hearty charge, "Stay the course. Get your power from this. Pull inspiration from this and PRESS ON! Someone needs your words, your song, your movement, your brush strokes, your keys, your gifts, to live through their most foreboding moment."

Please stay in the position of selfishly submitting your gift to the someone God has designed it for. When you do, something powerful shifts in the atmosphere. That is why I believe, darkness, despair, discouragement come blatantly and hard for creatives - especially those who call God - The Master Creator. You see life and light are magnified in our being and manifest in our art. When your words stop. When your voice goes quiet. When your brush won't hold color – the bullies are advancing against our spirit and minds and threaten heartbreak. Yet there is a moment when The Spirit above all things enables you yet again and you are transformed and elevated to stay the course. A great part of our transforming has to come in the consistent renewing of our spirits, our minds, and emotions. Renewing the presence and power of God within us must become a ritual as our oil of transformation is poured into our work.

Your battles illuminated through your creative gifts are for the someone waiting for your gift. Have you thought about her lately? Have you prayed for him lately? When there is no paparazzi, ticket sales, big names, applause - can you still pour your spirit and soul out for His glory? Can you do it for the someone counting on your stay?

Father, we submit our gifts, creativity, talents as unorthodox ministry to you, as radical, revolutionary transforming and glorifying works for The Kingdom and a bigger threat to the enemy's camp. In Jesus' name. Amen.

SUPPORTING SCRIPTURES FOR YOUR CONSIDERATION

Romans 12: 1 – 2
Second Peter 1:21
Ephesians 1: 11 and 4:1
Matthew 5:16
Psalm 51:10-12

Our Scriptural Mandate

Isaiah 45:5-8 (NKJV) - "I *am* the Lord, and *there is* no other; *There is* no God besides Me. I will gird you, though you have not known Me, That they may know from the rising of the sun to its setting. That *there is* none besides Me. I *am* the Lord, and *there is* no other; I form the light and create darkness, I make peace and create calamity; I, the Lord, do all these *things.*' "Rain down, you heavens, from above, And let the skies pour down righteousness; Let the earth open, let them bring forth salvation, And let righteousness spring up together. I, the Lord, have created it."

Romans 1:20 (NIV) – "For since the creation of the world God's invisible qualities—his eternal power and divine nature—have been clearly seen, being understood from what has been made, so that people are without excuse."

Affirmations

I consecrate my hands for the perfecting work of creating for God's glory.

I am well skilled to create works that are marvelous in The Savior's sight.

I am filled with all divine skills to do masterful works, for masterful purpose, with masterful meaning.

Whatever I put in my hands to create becomes anointed by The Potter's Hands.

I decree and declare that everything I create is exceedingly and abundantly blessed.

The Act of Creating Reflects God

Hillary Beth Koenig

Creator, You are worthy of all our praise. You alone are the Source of all that is light, truth, and good. From Genesis 1:1 through the gospel of John, we see You as the orchestrator of it all Thank you for the abilities and creativity You have bestowed upon humans to imitate You in these ways. When we make a beautiful work of art, compose a deeply moving song, create a strikingly attractive and warmly inviting space, design a beautiful and inspiring wardrobe, craft something from wood or metal to be used for generations, or write something that inspires generations to think and feel differently because of encountering our work, we not only invite growth and awe in the beholders, but point to You, Our Maker. Looking at beauty in this world, we see the seeds of The Gospel in so many things. Romans 1:20 says, "For his invisible attributes, namely, his eternal power and divine nature, have been clearly perceived, ever since the creation of the world, in the things that have been made. So, they are without excuse." All of the observable things reflect the invisible things of You, God.

As artists in any of the various roles that creativity may manifest in, the act of creating reflects who You are, Lord, and who You created us to be. May we learn how to navigate our self-expression

E. CLAUDETTE FREEMAN, EDITOR

and our expressing our love of what is good and beautiful, as it is of You.

Proverbs 22:29: "Do you see a man skillful in his work? He will stand before kings; he will not stand before obscure men."

We see great skill was bestowed upon man in the early days of the world Genesis 4:21-22, *"His brother's name was Jubal; he was the father of all who play stringed instruments and pipes. Zillah also had a son, Tubal-Cain, who forged all kinds of tools out of bronze and iron."*) We see it as well throughout history such as at the designing and building of the temple in Exodus 35:35, *"He has filled them with skill to do every sort of work done by an engraver or by a designer or by an embroiderer in blue and purple and scarlet yarns and fine twined linen, or by a weaver—by any sort of workman or skilled designer."* We reflect Him in the act of creating, making, shaping, forming, designing, and crafting things in the physical and observable world. Surely doing something extremely well gets the attention of others and is noted for all of history in many cases.

As a society, there have been times those in various fields have been idolized as people marvel over "the youngest," to accomplish something, "the oldest," to persist in something, "the first" in any various demographic or ethnic category, etc. When a Christ-follower stands out among the best, this means they have realized their skills, pursued excellence, and worked long and hard to finely tune their unique gifts and now they have the opportunity to glorify their Creator not only in the journey to becoming who they are, but also in their achievements before people who are seeking beauty, goodness, and truth. Success and accomplishments have their own dangers and temptations, but one who chooses to put the Lord first will recognize The One Who has filled them with this talent deserves all honor and glory, not just in lip-service, but in every action and interaction. Whether the product of our creative endeavors is specifically presenting a Christian subject or a more general subject about life (which we acknowledge all life has its origins in the Lord and so is tied to Him), excellence in technique and perseverance in the work can be as reflective as the final product.

Dear All-knowing, All-powerful, Ever-present, Loving Father, help us to remember that our talents, skills, accomplishments, and successes are only possible because of You. Let us not be blinded by the difficulties of our journey into thinking we can do these things on our own, but only by Your filling us. We pray in the name of Jesus. Amen.

Guard Our Hearts, Minds and Talent

Min. Miguel A. Guzman

> *"As each one has received a special gift, employ it in serving one another as good stewards of the multifaceted grace of God." (First Peter 4:10, NASB)*

> *"In his grace, God has given us different gifts for doing certain things well. So, if God has given you the ability to prophesy, speak out with as much faith as God has given you." (Romans 12:6, NLT)*

Dear Heavenly Father,

We exalt Your name above all names. You are our rock and firm foundation. In You we place our trust as we lay down our will for Yours. You have set us apart, equipping our minds with words, rhythm, and imagery to proclaim Your name in ways the entire world can comprehend so that they may encounter Your power and glory.

We know that all gifts come from You and those gifts and the calling upon our lives are irrevocable. (Romans 11:29) In that knowledge, we pray that You would provide wisdom and discernment so that these gifts may not be corrupted by selfish ambitions. We pray that the power and anointing of the Holy Spirit would cling to all we do, that all may experience Your wonder and encounter You.

We thank you for the gifts and talents You have given us. You have filled us with skill to do all kinds of works, from engraving, designing, and embroidering - all of us skilled workers and designers, (Exodus 35:35)) to name a few. You have given us tools to worship You. Our spirit shouts to You, Lord. We break out in praise and sing for joy. We sing our praise to You with the harp and melodious song, with trumpets and the sound of the ram's horn. We make a joyful symphony before You Lord, our King. (Psalm 98:4-6) With every instrument and every skill and artistic talents, we worship and exalt Your name.

You said in Genesis 1:27, that You created humankind in Your image. We were made by You and for You. In Your likeness, You created us with unlimited creativity and skill so that we can bring glory to Your name. So, we stand upon that promise. We pray that we may be filled by Your Spirit, anointed to create all kinds of works. We declare Your blessing over our barns and all we put our hands to. (Deuteronomy 28:8)

May You guard our hearts and minds in Christ Jesus, keeping us confident and humble in our creative spaces. May we not become arrogant, but remain meek, laying down our best before You, knowing that every good and perfect thing comes from You and You alone. May we decrease, so that You may increase within us. (John 3:30) Cover our thoughts and give us discernment to accept constructive criticism that will help us grow and rebuke the ridicule from others who wish to see us hide the talents You've called us to multiply. We declare no weapon formed against us shall prosper. (Isaiah 54:17) We demolish every pretension that exalts itself against the knowledge of God and we take captive

E. CLAUDETTE FREEMAN, EDITOR

every thought to make it obedient to Christ. (Second Corinthians 10:5) Keep us from anxiety. May we dwell on whatever is true, noble, right, pure, and admirable. (Philippians 4:8) As we dwell on Your goodness, may You continue to pour out Your Spirit on us.

Father, we lift every talent and gift before You. May our minds reflect the mind of Christ, our eyes see the world as You do and our hearts beat as one with Yours so that our creativity may be without limit as You are Alpha and Omega, the beginning, and the end. You are without boundaries.

We praise You for every talent and every gift You've given us, and we are blessed by who You are. May the works of our hands, the words of our mouths and the meditation of our hearts be pleasing to You and bring honor, glory, and power to Your name. In the mighty name of Jesus. Amen.

Declaration:

Everything God blesses me to create will manifest His assigned purpose in the Earth.

In Awe of Your Creation

Dr. Theresa Scott

"I will lift up mine eyes unto the hills from whence cometh my help. My help cometh from the Lord which made Heaven and Earth." (Psalm 121:1-2, NIV)

"O Lord my God You are great for You are clothed with honor and majesty." (Psalm 104:1, NIV)

Dear Heavenly Father, I come to You as the Creator of Heaven and Earth. You tell me in Your Word that the Earth is Yours, the fullness thereof, and they that dwell in it. (Psalm 24:1) I thank you for allowing me to be part of Your creation. I must agree with the psalmist David when he said he was fearfully and wonderfully made. (Psalm 139:14) How wonderful are the works of Your hands. You meticulously created and endowed me with gifts and talents. These abilities are awesome in my sight. Because of You, others have taken notice of what You have placed in me. These unique abilities have been used to tremendously bless others. Father open the way for the divine design of my life to manifest. Let the genius within me now be released. Reveal to me my perfect self-expression. I ask You to continue to open ways for more people to experience Your uniqueness in me. Grant me favor, opportunities and resources to reach them. Expand my territory. I only request that which is mine by divine right. May what You have endowed me with make room for me and bring me before great people. Cause this ability to bring comfort, love, and peace to those in need of it. It is my desire for them to experience You in all that I do. Thank you. In Jesus' name, Amen!

"My frame was not hidden from you when I was made in the secret place. When I was woven together in the depths of the Earth, your eyes saw my unformed body. All the days ordained for me were written in your book before one of them came to be." (Psalm 139:15-16)

"For we are God's workmanship, created in Christ to do good works, which God prepared in advance for us to do." (Ephesians 2:10)

Declaration:

I am fully equipped for the divine plan of my life. I will fearlessly take advantage of opportunities with the help of the Lord. I operate according to God's timetable. His agenda is my agenda. I am not my own. I have been bought with a price. Therefore, I submit myself to God alone.

No Small Task

Carol Lynne Wheeler

In Genesis 24:1-66, Abraham found himself aged and concerned about both his son and his legacy. It was important to him that his son Isaac find a wife. Abraham tasked his servant with finding a wife for Isaac but gave stipulations about it. Isaacs's future wife had to be from their country and not be a Canaanite. This would involve extensive travel, and during that time this type of travel was no small task. Abraham had his servant make an oath and the servant swore that he would do things exactly as he had been asked.

In verse 14 (NIV), we find the servant praying an extremely specific prayer to God. "May it be that when I say to a young woman, please let down your jar that I may drink, and she says drink, and I'll water your camels too-let her be the one you have chosen for your servant Isaac. By this I will know that You have shown kindness to my master." The Bible tells us that even before he could finish praying, Rebekah showed up with a jar on her shoulder.

The Bible describes Rebekah as a beautiful woman. I cannot imagine that Rebekah was any different than any of us who have prayed for a mate. Imagine Rebekah praying for a husband, and God sent her to the well to get water? It makes no sense that instead of God answering her prayer, He sends her to get water;

E. CLAUDETTE FREEMAN, EDITOR

except that with God, there are no small tasks. God is intentional; thus, what might seem insignificant to us is usually significant to Him.

In Genesis 24:17, after seeing Rebekah, the servant hurried to meet her and asked her for a little water from her jar. Rebekah responded with the kindness in which the servant had prayed for. How could Rebekah have known that the small act of kindness would lead to such a great blessing?

When we are seeking to operate under the will of God, we must be careful to pay attention to even the smallest details. There are times when the Holy Spirit of God will lead us to do something that might seem small and insignificant to us because we do not have the capacity to see the larger picture. We are tasked with doing this thing despite the lack of clarity we have. We, like Rebekah, will be the beneficiaries of blessings due to our obedience.

I have had such experiences on numerous occasions. On one occasion I was led to have a conversation with two older gentlemen in a restaurant. I was extremely uncomfortable and felt so odd about approaching them to talk. I struggled with it and told my husband how the Holy Spirit was leading me to do so. Finally, I approached them. After moments of conversation, it became clear why I had been led to do this. Because of their age, and the city we were in, I thought these two men had known my dad. They assured me they had not. I had given them my dad's first and last name and what he had done for a living; nothing. As I got ready to walk away embarrassed, one of the men told me they knew another man with that last name. Turns out they were speaking of my dad's brother, and they were old friends of his, but they fallen out of touch with him for a number of years. They had been looking to reconnect with him and my uncle as it turned out had been looking to reconnect with them. The men and my uncle had fought in Vietnam together. Being obedient to God and doing the small task of talking to these two men was the avenue God used to reconnect three old friends.

God can use the littlest things in what you create, in what you desire to create to bring us the biggest blessings. We must not be haughty but respond with obedience; understanding that when it comes to the work of the Holy Spirit, there are no small tasks.

God, I come before You today grateful that You still find use for me in Your Kingdom. Allow me to remain in awe of You and Your willingness to still find space for me. I take nothing for granted and if I should, please send me the swiftest reminders. Please never allow me to be outside of Your Will and always place it in my heart to be useful in Your Kingdom. In Jesus name I pray. Amen.

E. CLAUDETTE FREEMAN, EDITOR

A Grateful Heart

Metris Batts-Coley

> *"Make a joyful shout to the Lord, all you lands! Serve the Lord with gladness; Come before His presence with singing. Know that the Lord, He is God; It is He who has made us, and [b]not we ourselves; We are His people and the sheep of His pasture. Enter into His gates with thanksgiving, And into His courts with praise. Be thankful to Him and bless His name. For the Lord is good; His mercy is everlasting, And His truth endures to all generations." (Psalm 100:1-6, NKJV)*

> *"Have I not commanded you? Be strong and courageous. Do not be afraid; do not be discouraged, for the Lord your God will be with you wherever you go." (Joshua 1:9, NIV)*

Heavenly Father,

Creator of Heaven and Earth, thank you for breath and life. I rejoice in a new day to give You praise and thanks. I sing Your praise in my highest voice for Your Grace and Mercy. I thank you for the blessings in my life. I thank you for the second chances. I am grateful for my gifts and talents. How amazing it is to know that you specifically designed these gifts, talents, and a desire to create for me. I thank you that You graciously and powerfully use everything You instilled in me. Lord, I thank you for every opportunity and open door. May I always remember to possess each new land with boldness yet humility, knowing that You created the path for me. I will sing Your praise daily in my words, actions, and deeds. Lord, I thank you for another day filled with Your love, Your joy, Your peace.

Thank you for reminding me that the more I focus on Your Word the less I worry. Conquering fear grows my faith. I am created to create. I am gifted to me a gift. I am talented to share Your truth. Though there may be rough days, I will persist. I am an overcomer. I will not be discouraged. I will not give up. I may stumble. I may grumble but I will not quit. I cannot quit! Thank you for such determination to be who You created me to be and to create all that ordained me to.

Now God, Touch the hearts and minds of family and friends. Touch mind, body, blood, bone, and muscle of the sick and suffering. Touch the hearts of those grieving the loss of a loved one. Touch the hearts of the broken hearted. Touch the souls of those who do not know You. I speak these things in the name of Jesus The Christ and claim them to be so. Amen.

Declaration:

I create what God breathed into me each day for His glory and purpose.

Pure Imagination

By Min. Pam Shaw

> *Then God said, "Let Us make man in Our image,*
> *according to Our likeness; let them have dominion*
> *over the fish of the sea, over the birds of the air*
> *and over the cattle, over all the Earth and over*
> *every creeping thing that creeps on the Earth." So,*
> *God created man in His own image; the image of*
> *God He created him; male and female He created*
> *them. (Genesis 1:26-27)*

> *Out of the ground the Lord God formed every beast*
> *of the field and every bird of the air and brought*
> *them to Adam to see what he would call them. And*
> *whatever Adam called each living creature, that*
> *was its name. (Genesis 2:19)*

One of my favorite movies is the original *Willy Wonka and the Chocolate Factory*. Mr. Wonka sang a song entitled "Pure Imagination" (composers Leslie Bricusse and Anthony Newley, 1971). Here is an excerpt of those lyrics:

> *"There is no life I know*
> *To compare with pure imagination*
> *Living there you'll be free*
> *If you truly wish to be*

If you want to view paradise
Simply look around and view it
Anything you want to, do it
Want to change the world?
There's nothing to it
There is no life I know
To compare with pure imagination
Living there you'll be free
If you truly wish to be."

What pure genius, and I'm not just saying this because I love chocolate. This story follows a man and what he was able to create because of his imagination. His creativity knew no limits because he didn't allow himself, or anyone else for that matter, to be hindered by what could or couldn't be done. He fed his imagination. Think about all of the wonderful confectionary delights he concocted. As we saw throughout the movie, there were items that were still being perfected, but that didn't keep him from creating. And that creativity expanded beyond just making sweets, but gum that was a whole meal and even electronics that brought the goods right into your living room. The words of the song were truly brought to life, "Anything you want to, do it. Want to change the world? There's nothing to it." Willy Wonka changed the face of candy-making. There is nothing that can't be done, we simply have to put our minds to it.

Look around at creation. Look at the colors, the elements, the sounds, the smells, the textures, and tones of everyday life. Look at how seasons change and bring their own natural designs to the world year in and year out. It's amazing how so many of the same elements are all around us, yet they are all vastly different in their own way. Think about it. Even identical twins have something about them that makes them uniquely different from one another. What an amazing God!

E. CLAUDETTE FREEMAN, EDITOR

His imagination thought out the color patterns and every intricate detail of everything on the face of the Earth. His imagination was full of life, and it was vivid. And to think, within every one of us is the very same DNA of the Master Creator. He created us in His likeness and image, so we are not without the ability to think a thing and create it as well. And it doesn't matter how simple or complex. We have that very same ability to create.

Think about Adam. After every living thing was created by God, Adam was charged with giving them names. Can you imagine? Adam looking at the various creatures and deciding this would be the name for that particular animal or bird. And to think that to this very day, there are discoveries being made of creatures that we've never seen before. We are not without the ability to create.

The only limits that we truly possess, are the ones we possess. Our imaginations are gifts from God. Our ability to see dirt, water, and colorful rocks and decide they are the best M & M mud pies in the neighborhood worked well for us as little children; how much more so even now? That blank computer screen before you is the starting block to the story that will take a young mind to a far-away land. That blank canvas is the next piece of artwork to challenge the perception of an avid art collector. That blank sheet of paper will hold the notes of the next song that will cause someone to hope again. The microphone. The stage. The instrument. The ingredients. It's within you to create. Why? Because God created you, and everything He creates is good.

Father, thank you for the creativity You have ingrained in me. Thank you for the ability to put my hands to anything and greatness manifesting from them. I pull down every negative, mind blocking thought into captivity, and I release the free flow of my thoughts and imagination in You. Truly, I can do all things through Christ and Yes, Lord I will. In Jesus' name, Amen.

Affirmations

I will not neglect my gift. I prophecy that it will prophecy and minister to all who encounter it.

Whatever I create, I do with everything in me and for Him. My work is for the Lord.

I am God's great handiwork, He created me to create to complete His good works.

I am part of a heritage of creators of empires, kingdoms, industries. I was created to create.

I declare that my gifts fall from the Throne Room of Heaven to bless me perpetually.

God's Awesome Handiwork

Min. Anita Faye Wilson

> *"You are worthy, O Lord, to receive glory and honor and power; For You created all things, And by Your Will they exist and were created." (Revelation 4:11, NLT)*

Eternal God, our Father. The Maker of Heaven and Earth. Awesome Ruler. I come before Your throne of grace with a humble heart and a contrite spirit pouring out my heart to You who has given me life and the privilege of prayer. I praise You for all that You are. You are Jehovah Rophe, our Healer. You are Jehovah Shalom, our Peace. You are Jehovah Jireh, our Provider. You are the Great I Am. You have all power in Your hands. I can come and cast all of my cares at Your feet. I am grateful that You love me more than I could ever love myself. You have so many wonderful attributes, I do not have enough words or tongues to express them all or declare my thanks. I pause in the midst of Your excellent grace and thank you for being an awesome Creator.

You brought everything into existence and without You nothing would be. Everywhere I look, I see Your awesome handywork. All throughout life and everything I do I still see Your hand at work. The creative power that You have You gave to us. You gave us the ability to reason. You gave us gifts that come without repentance. You gave us a mind to sort through logic and gain understanding. You gave us insight. You continue to give us dreams and visions. I praise You, Oh God, for the ability to envision my visions and to paint a blank canvas of what You have given me. Everything that I do is to magnify and glorify You. I was created to do Your Will. You foreordained and predestined the creativity in my DNA. I can't help but be creative because I am made in Your image, and You are The Creator of all and rule over all things. Ephesians 2:10 says, *"For we are His workmanship, created in Christ Jesus for good works, which God prepared beforehand that we should walk in them."* God, I ask you to cover every thought and to make clear everything that I dream. For the visions and dreams that I have are only a glimpse of what You are able to do by the power that You have imparted into me. Ephesians 3:20 says, *"Now to Him who is able to do exceedingly abundantly above all that we ask or think, according to the power that works in us."* I pray that through the creative work of my hands ordained by You that lives are changed, the captives are set free, and that anyone I come in to contact with is blessed beyond measure. I am nothing without You, God. And anything that I put my hand to is nothing without Your stamp of approval or Your trademark.

Thank you, God for believing in me enough to save me from my sins and giving me an identity with You in Christ Jesus. Thank you for giving me a purpose and a destiny. I promise to always stay true to that for which You have laid ahold of me. And I will forever give You all of the honor, glory, and praise, in Jesus' mighty and holy name. Amen!

Declarations:

I declare that I am your child made in your image. And anything I touch is blessed. I declare that I am fearfully and wonderfully made. Your handywork in me will bless lives long after I'm gone. I declare that because Your hand is on me and all that I do I will always operate in a spirit of excellence.

E. CLAUDETTE FREEMAN, EDITOR

Your Charge for the Assignment

NTOZAKE'S WISDOM

E. Claudette Freeman

Ntozake - she who comes with her own things. Shange – she who walks like a lion. The poet, playwright, professor best known for the choreopoem "FOR COLORED GIRLS WHO HAVE CONSIDERED SUICIDE/WHEN THE RAINBOW IS ENUF" died in her sleep Saturday morning, October 27, 2018. Her death sat me down for a moment. I had the honor of studying under Ntozake at the Atlantic Center for the Arts during a Master Artists-in-Residency program. The weeks spent with her were intriguing, challenging, crazy. We stood in circles and made primal noises. She'd probe, we'd respond, she'd probe deeper.

During that artists-in-residency, Ntozake said something to me that forced me to rethink who I am as a writer and why I write. She declared that (and I hold tight to her declaration), "Every word you write should live. They should give life. They should give breath. They should move hearts, souls, mountains. They should dance. They should move. They should scream I AM HERE! If they don't, why are you writing them?"

What happens with God's creative people that we go from that kind of fire and passion to looking at the vastness of gifting in our hands, minds, spirit and seeing a valley of dry bones? (Ezekiel 37:1–6)

The bigger question for His creative purpose holders, is what is causing your bones to dry in the valley? Failure to be disciplined? Failure to strengthen your gift? Failure to honor the anointing in your creativity? Failure to learn from the hard things? He said, she said discouragement? Waiting to hear God when you won't seek Him?

Your bones are dying in the valley. That book dying in the valley is to be a teaching tool revolutionizing Kingdom work. That play dying in the valley is to shatter traditional spiritual and social contexts. That painting clinging to life in the valley is prophetic and designed to create conversations that will raise a generation of warriors. But they're becoming dry bones. Prophet of God – before you speak to the bones in the valley, prophesy to the one who holds the gift and cast down the intrinsic belief systems that are casting you down. When you do, God promises in verses 11 through 14 of Ezekiel 37:

"Then he said to me: "Son of man, these bones are the people of Israel. They say, 'Our bones are dried up and our hope is gone; we are cut off.' Therefore, prophesy and say to them: 'This is what the Sovereign Lord says: My people, I am going to open your graves and bring you up from them; I will bring you back to the land of Israel. Then you, my people, will know that I am the Lord, when I open your graves and bring you up from them. I will put my Spirit in you, and you will live, and I will settle you in your own land. Then you will know that I the Lord have spoken, and I have done it, declares the Lord.'"

Speak movement, life, breath, assignment, hope and the Spirit of The Living God into that you have been divinely chosen to create and send it forth to settle the truth of God in the land.

Father, we thank you for the exceeding great army of our talents, gifts, creativity coming to life with fierce and loud rattling, with breath of life, with intention and purpose. We declare it to me so, in the name of Jesus, we pray. Amen.

Supporting Scriptures:

Exodus 35:31-35
Ezekiel 37: 1-14
First Timothy 4:14
Colossians 3:23

Creative Flows in God

Regina Griffin

> "He has filled them with skill to do all kinds of work as engravers, designers, embroiderers in blue, purple and scarlet yarn and fine linen, and weavers=all of them skilled workers and designers." (Exodus 35:35, NIV)

Dear God,

We come to You first giving thanks for Your amazing love that we experience every day. As we look around at this world that You created, we are reminded of the beauty of Your works, of Your plans, and how all things flow according to Your divine plan and will. Thank you for the wind that blows across our faces reminding us of the ability to feel and walk in faith. Just as we can't see the wind, we often can't see Your wonderful works, but we walk in faith knowing that You have a design greater than we can ever begin to construct on our own. We come humbly before You, seeking and trusting in You to allow Your gifts to flow through us. We ask that You lay Your powerful hand and breathe life into our writings. We ask that You paint Your love upon our canvases. Lord, we ask that Your love, Your power, and Your outstanding presence speaks through our creative gifts and inspires others. Lord, we thank you in advance for allowing our songs, our works, our presence, and our talents to transform the lives of everyone that encounters them. Lord, we ask You to give us the vision and the guidance to execute the plan for Your glory.

Father may this prayer marinate in our spaces, as we give thanks for the gifts that You have bestowed upon us. Often times, we don't know how to effectively hone our talents for Your glory. Lord, in those times remind of Colossians 3:23, *"Whatever you do, work at it with all your heart, as working for the Lord, not for human masters."* Let our gifts flow with all our hearts. Father, we keep our ears and hearts open to You daily. Speak, Thou Great King in a simple verse from a song that paints a beautiful picture and pours life into our weary souls which may feel hopeless. God plant the seed and we'll be the fruit of Your grand plan. We thank you. We trust you. We know your plan is always greater than ours, and we love you. Amen.

Declaration:

God will get the praise for the beauty that flows through me and flows into the lives of others.

An Enduring Love

Britany A. Brooks

> *"Cast your cares on the Lord and He will sustain you; He will never let the righteous be shaken."* (Psalm 55:22, NIV)

Dear Heavenly Father,

We give You all the honor and the glory, for You are good! Your love and mercy endureth forever! Let those in the Creative Arts ministries say, "His mercy endures forever!" Let every creative entrepreneur in Christ Jesus say, "His Word endures forever!"

Father, it's no secret that the enemy is against every plan that You have for Your children. It's no secret that the enemy aims to form weapons against our minds and ideas, which are tied to our purpose for our lives. Lord, it's no secret that the enemy tries to generate fear in each of us. It's no secret that the father of lies, aims to manipulate us into thinking, he has the power. But Father, Your Word already said, *"For God hath not given us the spirit of fear; but of power, and of love, and of a sound mind."* (Second Timothy 1:7) So, by The Word of our All-Powerful and Almighty God, we declare that no weapon formed against His children shall prosper! And every tongue which rises against us in judgment shall be condemned! (Isaiah 54:17)

Mighty God of all mankind! May Your children never allow fear to be the driving force; for You are always with us. May we be not dismayed, for You are our Jehovah Nissi! You will fight for us! And we shall hold our peace. Lord, You will strengthen and help us. So may we keep Your instruction on our hearts.

ABBA! You are a GENEROUS GOD! The GREAT I AM. The NEVER-ENDING SUPPLY! So, Lord, we are confident that when Your children come to You, our supply will never run out. For You have declared in Your Word (John 6:35), *"I am the Bread of Life. Whoever comes to me will never go hungry, and whoever believes in me will never be thirsty."* So may You bless us abundantly, so that in all things at all times, having all that we need, we will abound in every good work. Father, You have created us so beautifully, so valuable, and purposeful through Your image. So may Your wonderful beings, never forget that our self-sufficiency is in You; and we need not to rely on this world. You are our Good Shepherd! We will never lack!

"And we know that in all things God works for the good of those who love Him, who have been called according to His purpose." (Romans 8:28)

Mighty God, may we, Your children, never forget that there is purpose in our consistency. There will be a reward at the end when we persevere in Your good works. For as the Scripture says, *"You need to persevere so that when you have done the will of God, you will receive what He has promised."* (Hebrews 10:36) And we are confident that *"those who hope in the Lord will renew their strength. They will soar on wings like eagles; they will run and not grow weary; they will walk and not be faint."* (Isaiah 40:31)

Father, may we be empowered by Your Word; for it only takes faith as small as a mustard seed. So may we reap a fruitful and beautiful harvest, that's beyond what the mind can conceive. May the grace and love of the Lord Jesus be with us. Amen.

Declaration:

I will not allow the plans of the enemy, to derail me from God's purpose! I will not allow fear to cripple God's plans for my life!

No Fear

By Min. Pam Shaw

For God has not given us a spirit of fear; but of love and of power and of a sound mind. (Second Timothy 1:7)

While I have been an avid daydreaming writer and storyteller all my life, my professional career as an actress did not begin until 2013. I can remember my very first play in elementary school. I played Mother Nature and our task as an ensemble was to get the month of April to cry so that May could bring flowers. I vaguely remember being told I would be playing that role. I'm sure I was nervous, but at that early age our nerves are made of steel, so we just roll with it in our carefree way. However, that part of me lay dormant until I led the drama group at my then local church as a writer/director. I enjoyed being behind the scenes. Being onstage and/or in front of large crowds brought multiple levels of anxiety upon me. In my mind, I wasn't good enough to be on anyone's stage. Today, that is laughable because I made it onstage once at the very last minute due to a lead not being able perform. I learned the lines during the seven-hour trip to Brevard, North Carolina where we were scheduled to perform. Talk about being nervous with higher levels of anxiety, but I made it through, and the show was a tremendous success. Yet, still, that part of me lay dormant.

Fast forward several years, marriage and several children later, my two oldest girls are in middle school trying out for the basketball team. I was completely inspired by them and their drive. They weren't among the taller girls, but they had drive and fierce determination. That touched something in me and for whatever reason, I found myself submitting my information for an audition. For years, I had watched other people live out dreams and take steps into careers and passions that drove them. I counted myself out plenty of times because I didn't feel I was educated enough or pretty enough or talented enough to cause even the slightest ripple in someone's thought concerning me. It didn't help that I was extremely introverted and self-conscious either, but that was what I was dealing with. That is until I found myself standing on a stage auditioning for a professional show and after singing the director asked, "Where have you been hiding all of this time?" While I laughed and said "church", I know what the honest answer was and had been for a long time.

I had been hiding in fear. Fear is paralyzing and the ultimate weapon in the arsenal of warfare against us. Fear can cause thoughts to run rampant in our minds, telling us who we aren't and all of the things we are incapable of doing. Fear will have us look at people, who are just like us, and think so lowly of ourselves, when in all actuality there is greatness inside of each of us. Fear will have us to forget that we are all fearfully and wonderfully made. Each one unique, gifted, and talented in our own way. We are so busy comparing ourselves and measuring ourselves against everyone else, we miss developing our own style and voice. I had actually lost my voice, who I was and who I could have shaped out to be early on. Fear had me in a vice. That was until that audition in 2013.

Something awakened in me that had been laying there waiting to be watered and nurtured. It never went anywhere because God created it in me. I had to get tired of watching from the sidelines and downplaying the abilities that were there. I sold myself so short because I thought I *had* to go to school for it or because I thought I needed to know the ins and outs to the letter in order to succeed. Do you know that if you ask for wisdom in a thing, God is faithful to provide it? The gifting and talent were already within me. The wisdom to use it was released upon me and I was able to audition for and book other roles after that first one.

We must learn to take every fearful thought into captivity unto the obedience of Christ. Pull those thoughts in until you start speaking right. It's okay to be nervous about whatever you're venturing into, but don't allow yourself to function or cower in fear. Nurture and make use of the gifts and talents the Lord has blessed you with. Stop comparing yourself and what you feel you are able to do with everyone else. He created you with a style and voice that is all your own. Be courageous in who He has made you to be and with what He has gifted you to do. The world is waiting for you.

Father, we thank you for the gifts and talents that you have blessed us with. We bind the spirit of fear that would cause us not to move forward. We thank you for wisdom, courage, and creativity. It is because of Christ Jesus that we are strengthened to do all things and for that we give You praise. In Jesus' name, Amen.

Developing in His Presence

Dr. Theresa Scott

> *"Commit to the Lord whatever you do, and your plans will succeed." (Proverbs 16:3, NLT)*

> *"I will instruct you and teach you in the way you should go; I will counsel you and watch over you." (Psalm 32:8, NIV)*

Lord, You are my light and my salvation. You are the strength of my life. Blessed be the name of the Lord from this time forth and ever more. From the rising of the sun unto the going down of the same the Lord's name is to be praised. I will bless You while I live. I will lift up my hands in Your name.

Dear Heavenly Father thank you for allowing me to come into Your presence where I can worship You in Spirit and in Truth. Thank you for always being available to me in my good and bad times. You say in Your Word that Your ears are attentive to my prayers. (Psalm 34:15) Therefore, I come to The One Who is all-knowing and full of wisdom. You have entrusted me with a gift to create in the Earth. I ask You to give me the tongue and the hands of the learned for this gift and for Your purpose. Cause my mind to understand the skilled, economic, and financial aspects of the talent You've blessed me with. Help me to comprehend and utilize marketing, promotional, and social media platforms. Lead me to the right people with this expertise. Let me not be deceived by unscrupulous, dishonest, and selfish people. Father, this gift and spirit of creativity is because of You. It will be nurtured and released with integrity and moral rectitude. I trust You as my Source.

I ask You to release all that is needed for this creative enterprise to operate sufficiently. Cause the right people to make room for me. Develop my people skills. Help me to communicate about that which I have created in an understandable and respective way. Grant me discernment to know what is and is not of You. Thank you for entrusting this creative gift to me. In Jesus' name, Amen!

Declaration:

Everything prepared for me before the foundation of the world that pertains to my life and creativity comes to me now. I will not be denied, nor will I accept substitutes.

Oil Flowing Like Manna

Min. Shaqwana Morrel Reed

"I prayed to the Lord my God and confessed: «Lord, the great and awesome God, who keeps his covenant of love with those who love him and keep his commandments." (Daniel 9:4; NIV)

Dear Most Gracious and Heavenly Father, I bow before Your presence in humility. I thank you for Your unconditional love, Your unwavering grace, and Your unmatchable mercy. God, I praise Your name because there is no other name above Yours and no other name deserves Your glory! God as I lift you up, let me decrease so that Your words can speak through me.

Lord, I come to You, laying my creative gifts at the altar. Lord, I know that you have ordained each of us to walk in a specific area and that even includes the creative purpose that You have chosen for us. Your Word says in Jeremiah 1:5 that you knew us before we even entered our mothers' wombs and that you set us apart. So, God, I thank you for every area of our lives that You have chosen. Lord I pray that as we get into that secret place with You, that we will not only hear Your instructions for our lives but obediently purse them.

God, I thank you that as I choose to be obedient to You, You are making everything that I touch prosper. I am standing on Your Word. Matthew 6:33 has promised that all I have to do is seek after The Kingdom and Your righteousness and You will give me all that I need and even my heart's desires. Lord, I thank you that even as I conduct business around the creativity You have placed in my hands, I don't have to chase after fame or fortune in order to prosper. As I chase You, You will supply all my needs. As I make Your name great, You will reign down prosperity

Father teach me what I have been created to do so that I may please You and fulfill my purpose in the land. God, I know it may not look like what the world thinks it should look like. God, I know that many may not agree with where You are leading me or what it should look like. But Lord as long as I am pleasing You, nothing else matters. When the world looks like it is shutting down, my creativity will thrive because of my obedience. Psalm 23 reminds me that You are my shepherd and because of it I shall not want.

May Your oil flow down like manna from heaven and begin to overtake my gifts so that they may prosper. I pray that every business transaction around my gifting glorifies You. I pray that my creative business will be a light in an industry of darkness to show the world that You are God and that You are good to those who follow You and obey.

Father God, I just thank you for loving me enough to impart Your wisdom into my heart, my life, my hands, my business, and all that I touch. Lord, I ask that You to continue to walk with me so that I may be pleasing in Your sight. In Jesus' name, amen.

Declaration:

I decree and declare that the blessings of Abraham are over my life. Because I am an heir with Jesus, I am able to prosper and to break the yoke of bondage. I am anointed to break strongholds and allow generations after me to walk in the overflow of God.

Giver of All Good Things

Hillary Beth Koenig

Lord, we could never praise You enough for all of the wonderful things You have done for us from the beginning of creation to the sacrifice of Your Son for the forgiveness of sins and continue to do every day. We praise You for the promise of redemption being completely fulfilled and all things reconciled in the future, and we know our hope is in You alone.

Until that time, may we cry, as 1 Chronicles 16: 34 says, *"Oh, give thanks to the Lord, for He is good! For His mercy endures forever."* For we know that Your goodness is what we long for, as Psalm 107:8-9 says, *"Oh, that men would give thanks to the Lord for His goodness, and for His wonderful works to the children of men! For He satisfies the longing soul and fills the hungry soul with goodness."* Oh, what a picture, to be filled with goodness tracing right back to the Maker of our very souls. Surely in a world full of brokenness and despair, we see the difference a filled soul can make.

Lord, we realize that some look on good things and ignore the deeper truths that can be drawn from these gifts, instead focusing on the gifts themselves. It's easy in our fallen nature to find something good and cling to it. As Christians, may we realize, *"Every good gift and every perfect gift is from above, and comes down from The Father of lights, with whom there is no variation or shadow of turning,"* (James 1:17).

Let us not fall victim to even unintentionally worshipping or idolizing the good gifts of The Father instead of The Father himself, or we will miss the best in life, and the point of eternal life – being in the presence of the Lord forever.

Father, I commit back into Your hands every good gift You have given – whether talent, the work of my hands, the people in my life, the role models and mentors, family and friends and supporters, or possessions, and even passions. Remind me that anything good in this life is from You and belongs to You.

"I will meditate on the glorious splendor of Your majesty, and on Your wondrous works. Men shall speak of the might of Your awesome acts, and I will declare Your greatness. They shall utter the memory of Your great goodness and shall sing of Your righteousness." (Psalm 145:5-7)

During the creation of the world, God looked at each point in creation and said that it was good – this is a repetitive theme through the entire first two chapters of Genesis. All He created was good, as it was from Him and by Him and through Him that it came into being. God then created you, as well, according to Psalm 139. And so, you were given a unique set of talents – there are things you are, and do, and create that are good things. When you use those talents to create something good, and new, and beautiful, you have the opportunity to lift the eyes of your audience to dwell on goodness that has come from God. You get to invite others, *"Oh, taste and see that the Lord is good; blessed is the man who trusts in Him!"* as Psalm 34:8 conveys. What have you tasted that caused you to realize that the Lord is so good?

When you give Him honor and glory, there are some who might accuse you of doing that for show and attention and self-honor, but your character will back you up in your genuine heart for serving the Lord. As you care for your community, give to those in need, and humble yourself in prayer, your patterns will reflect more of His goodness in you. He is the giver of your talents, dreams, passions, opportunities, and relationships. He is The Orchestrator of all of the things that have come together to make you who you are, from the initial creation, to the cross, to your life as it is today. *"He has made everything beautiful in its time. Also, he has put eternity into man's heart, yet so that he cannot find out what God has done from the beginning to the end,"* (Ecclesiastes 3:11).

The soul longs for such goodness and beauty that an artist in their field can capture and share in their own unique way. What a gift this is to bring to others, acknowledging The Source of all good things!

Lord, may we never cease to rejoice in You, The Giver of Life, and all things that are good in this life and the life to come. May we seek to find You in all of the aspects of our lives and praise You unceasingly. Amen.

The Gift of Creativity

Evangelist Annette L. Anderson

"But from there you will search again for the LORD your God. And if you search for him with all your heart and soul, you will find him." (Deuteronomy 4:29, NLT)

Our Lord and Savior, we give You glory, honor and power, for You have created all things, and by Your Word creation was born. Bless now these Earthly creators and all their creations.

Almighty God and wonderful Creator, empower us to recognize the creativity that You've created in each person. Enable us to celebrate the difference of God's great gifts in His people. Give us the ability to embrace our difference to its fullness. Lord, equip us with what we need to accomplish the creative abilities, that You have so graciously bestowed upon us. First, give us the strength to acknowledge the gifts. Secondly, give us the power and the ability to go forward with Your gifts. Finally, remind us that creativity is limitless and there are no boundaries to what can be accomplished when we seek You first. Regardless of the situations, give us strength to overcome anything that will hinder or stifle our creativity.

We acknowledge the perfect gift of creativity, knowing that all gifts come from You God. The Bible states in James 1:17 *"Every good gift and every perfect gift is from above, and cometh down from The Father of lights, with whom is no variableness, neither shadow of turning."* We sometimes feel inadequate as the vessel that God had chosen to use, with our frailties, but God does not call the qualified, God qualifies the called. He will equip us. He will speak for us. He will provide the help we need. He will use us. As we journey in this life, the key to our relationship with God, is trusting in His Divine plan, being confident that He's sovereign and will always act in our best interest, working it out at the right moment.

Please give me the power to overcome fear that impedes me from engaging in my creativity. I believe The Creator has made me to be creative, but I still struggle with the gift He has given me. As the writer said in Mark 9:24, Lord, I believe but help my unbelief! Please help us to overcome our fear and anxiety. Allow us to change our thoughts and mindsets, so that we can be open to hear Your Word. Isaiah 55:8 states, *"For my thoughts are not your thoughts, neither are your ways my ways, saith the Lord."* So, God I am so glad you see past where we are, to see where You have called us to be.

God, I thank you for Your mercy and grace. Thank you that You've been able to give me hope, even when I feel hopeless. Thank you for the creativity that You give me and Your amazing power that continues to work in my life. Thank you that You've now given me strength to walk into my purpose. Thank you for Your love that is beyond any love I've ever experienced. Thank you for Your promises that You have spoken my life, help me to trust Your Word and believe that it is true. Open my eyes to see the creativity You've given me, and the plan You have for me, and my ability to walk into my destiny.

Declaration:

Creativity is my ability to walk into the uniqueness, which was designed just for me. I pray, believe, and persevere!

Your Charge for the Assignment

ARE YOU PREPARED FOR THE HELP YOU'RE PRAYING FOR?

E. Claudette Freeman

There are several actors whose talent I admire. Some I know, some I do not. Of those I know three come to mind: Margarette Joyner, Karen Stephens and Daryl Patrice. They are not containable talents. What I mean is they are not likely to be typecast or confined to one type of stage or genre. They mix it up. They take their gifts to the scripts and troupes that intrigue them, and they can intrigue in. They have no box that they carefully place their creativity in, and I admire that. Their territory moves and expands because they allow their gift to do the same - unhindered, unafraid, and unashamed.

When we realize that we pray for major platforms in our creativity but then consistently wear minor league behavior we put shackles on the God who created the whole universe in a few days. We put Him in a box, yet the talents, gifts that we are anointed to carry fills the Earth. Seek a God with no boundaries and become a creative vessel with no boundaries but purpose based on God's promises and God's expansive territories, realms, lands, huge doors, and unbelievable opportunities.

The challenges for God's creatives to disband the physical and metaphorical boxes that try to contain us:

- ➢ Negate the boundaries that restrict God.
- ➢ Trust God each week to place your creativity in unfamiliar territory.
- ➢ Sacrifice every I don't have, I'm not good enough, I never have notion daily.
- ➢ Release that thing - that bit of arrogance thing – that locks you in a land because you want to be seen where you want to be seen.
- ➢ Your territory may NOT be where your comfort is, choose which one serves your God purpose.
- ➢ Give back to God an honorable portion of what He's given you and EXPECT His blessings (in fact, open an OVERFLOW ACCOUNT at your financial institution for His abundance).
- ➢ Change your language. Stop telling God where and how your blessing needs to be; pack for where your trust will create a blessed place for your creativity to explode.

Dear God, enlarge my territory, shatter my limited ideas of where Your gift can flourish, grant me bigger opportunities and open bigger doors than I could fathom. Blow on every project and send Your creativity in me to every corner of the universe. I cover these words in the Blood of Christ and it is in His name that I pray. Amen.

SCRIPTURES FOR YOUR CONSIDERATION

First Chronicles 4:9-10
Deuteronomy 28: 1-8
Psalm 37:3-33; 78:41-43 and 52-56

E. CLAUDETTE FREEMAN, EDITOR

Affirmations

I am the legacy of The Supreme God, who created the Heavens and the Earth. His creativity is my DNA.

I am assured by The Word, that my work will put me before royalty.

I am full of the works God has endowed me. I must release my work into the Earth.

I do not create to the pattern of this world. I create to transform, renew, and show His good, pleasing, and perfect will.

I pour out every good and witty idea that God has poured into me. My creations are synchronized with His.

My Creative Mission

We must be intentional about what we want the work we design to do. Each story, each painting, each stitch of fabric, etc. must have a specific mission. Create a mission statement for who you are as a creative molded in The Father's hand for such a time as this.

_____
_____
_____
_____
_____
_____
_____
_____
_____
_____
_____
_____
_____
_____
_____
_____
_____
_____
_____
_____
_____
_____
_____

E. CLAUDETTE FREEMAN, EDITOR

My Creative Vision

When you close your eyes, when you fill yourself with child-like wonder and curiosity, where does what you create take you? There is the authentic and genuine place of your vision. Vulnerably and without apology write your vision, make it plain and then run with it knowing that God loves, respects, and honors your innovation.

_____
_____
_____
_____
_____
_____
_____
_____
_____
_____
_____
_____
_____
_____
_____
_____
_____
_____
_____
_____
_____

My Prayer for My Gifting

_____
_____
_____
_____
_____
_____
_____
_____
_____
_____
_____
_____
_____
_____
_____
_____
_____
_____
_____
_____
_____
_____
_____
_____
_____
_____
_____
_____
_____
_____

E. CLAUDETTE FREEMAN, EDITOR

My Weekly Fast

Fasting, when added to intentional prayer, is a powerful tool to gain God's desire, direction, covering, increased anointing and so much more.

As creative artists, fasting is critical to assure that you are creating what is wonderfully pleasing to The Father and able to transcend a myriad of woes, dogmas, disbelief and more to open a door for ministry, encouragement, and life transformation.

Hopefully this sheet will allow you to dig in and turn down, turn off and release something to gain more of The Holy Spirit.

Day/Date:_____

Fasting about: _____
_____
_____
_____

Focus scriptures: _____
_____
_____
_____

What God spoke:

_____
_____
_____
_____
_____
_____
_____
_____
_____
_____
_____
_____
_____
_____
_____
_____
_____
_____
_____
_____
_____
_____
_____
_____
_____
_____
_____
_____
_____
_____

My Weekly Fast

Fasting, when added to intentional prayer, is a powerful tool to gain God's desire, direction, covering, increased anointing and so much more.

As creative artists, fasting is critical to assure that you are creating what is wonderfully pleasing to The Father and able to transcend a myriad of woes, dogmas, disbelief and more to open a door for ministry, encouragement, and life transformation.

Hopefully this sheet will allow you to dig in and turn down, turn off and release something to gain more of The Holy Spirit.

Day/Date:_____

Fasting about: _____
_____
_____
_____

Focus scriptures: _____
_____
_____
_____

What God spoke:

_____

_____

_____

_____

_____

_____

_____

_____

_____

_____

_____

_____

_____

_____

_____

_____

_____

_____

_____

_____

_____

_____

_____

_____

_____

_____

_____

_____

_____

_____

_____

_____

My Weekly Fast

Fasting, when added to intentional prayer, is a powerful tool to gain God's desire, direction, covering, increased anointing and so much more.

As creative artists, fasting is critical to assure that you are creating what is wonderfully pleasing to The Father and able to transcend a myriad of woes, dogmas, disbelief and more to open a door for ministry, encouragement, and life transformation.

Hopefully this sheet will allow you to dig in and turn down, turn off and release something to gain more of The Holy Spirit.

Day/Date:_____

Fasting about: _____

_____

_____

_____

Focus scriptures: _____

_____

_____

_____

What God spoke:

_____
_____
_____
_____
_____
_____
_____
_____
_____
_____
_____
_____
_____
_____
_____
_____
_____
_____
_____
_____
_____
_____
_____
_____
_____
_____
_____
_____
_____
_____
_____

My Weekly Fast

Fasting, when added to intentional prayer, is a powerful tool to gain God's desire, direction, covering, increased anointing and so much more.

As creative artists, fasting is critical to assure that you are creating what is wonderfully pleasing to The Father and able to transcend a myriad of woes, dogmas, disbelief and more to open a door for ministry, encouragement, and life transformation.

Hopefully this sheet will allow you to dig in and turn down, turn off and release something to gain more of The Holy Spirit.

Day/Date:_____

Fasting about: _____
_____
_____
_____

Focus scriptures: _____
_____
_____
_____

What God spoke:

_____
_____
_____
_____
_____
_____
_____
_____
_____
_____
_____
_____
_____
_____
_____
_____
_____
_____
_____
_____
_____
_____
_____
_____
_____
_____
_____
_____
_____
_____
_____

E. CLAUDETTE FREEMAN, EDITOR

Closing Declaration

Child of God,

Who creates according to the power of The Holy Spirit; every good, beautiful, and perfect thing that is created through you is the manifestation of all things good, beautiful, and perfect from The Father of Creation.

Create continually in obedience to God and reside in His Divine blessings.

Be bold, courageous, and even fearful. Yet, create and minister through your works and be strengthened by God as you do so.

You are a royal and peculiar artist called to be a gift to His purpose and plans according to His sovereignty. Go forth in your anointing!

E. Claudette Freeman

The Contributors

Shaqwana M Reed lives in Tampa, FL. She is a wife, mom, author, certified "wife" coach, mentor, and entrepreneur. Shaqwana's main goal in life to show people that with God you can get through anything and once you make it through each situation, you become empowered to help others do the same. Shaqwana wrote and published her first book Recipes to a Healed and Happy Life in 2019. In the book she shares how to forgive and find your happy again. As the owner of S to C Edible Delights, LLC, she spreads love through baking.

Miguel A. Guzman is a Newyorican who grew up in Central Florida and now resides in Sunny Isles Beach, FL with Lina, his beautiful wife of 14 years. As a Certified Audio Engineer, he loves to produce music in his free time. He actively volunteers in ministry, leading the production team at 1 Name Church, in South Florida. He is also a travel and foodie aficionado, always looking to explore new territories, dishes and sharing his love of God and people.

Dr. Theresa Scott is a prophet, teacher, and empowerment speaker. She has been saved over 40 years. She ministers with her husband (Apostle Dr. Richard Scott) at Grow in Grace Worship Center, Delmar, Maryland. (www.gigwc.com). Dr. Scott received her Doctor of Divinity degree from Spirit of Truth Institute, Richmond, VA; Master of Christian Education and Bachelor of Biblical Studies degrees from H. E. Wood Bible Institute & Theological Seminary, Alexandria, VA. Dr. Scott is the author of PERFECTING MOMENTS and THE JOURNEY. Dr. Scott comes with a wealth of experience and wisdom in walking with God. She is a sought-out speaker in workshops, conferences, and intimate settings. Her passion is for people to accept themselves and walk in the power of their individuality.

Regina Griffin was born and raised in Meridian, Mississippi, she is a mother of three. Her loves include writing in diverse styles, and technology, including cybersecurity and programming. Regina is an avid believer in expressing love, living a positive lifestyle, encouraging others, and applying knowledge that impacts others, not only self. She can be found blogging, reading, tinkering with technology, enjoying family, and cooking up creative ideas to soothe her entrepreneurial spirit.

Min. Pamela Shaw is a native of Richmond, Virginia. She has been married to Omar Shaw for twenty years and together they have five children. Pamela enjoys spending time with her family, reading, writing, singing, and acting. While being on the stage has been a life changing, saving grace for her, Pamela thoroughly enjoys directing as well. She is thankful for her start at Virginia Repertory Theatre and grateful for her growth at The Heritage Ensemble Theatre Company. She is the founder and pastor of 4th Wall Love Connect Ministries, an outreach ministry where she has been serving since 2017. Pamela is the Executive Administrative Manager of Pivot with P.A.M. Pivot Administrative Management™, a virtual administrative consultant business.

Carol Lynne Wheeler - 1969, the year of the Stonewall Riots, Woodstock, Sesame Street, and this author. Carol is a writer, a mother, a bundle of light, student of The Bible, and a woman on a mission to heal as many women as she can. She is an inspirational teacher, spreading authentic truths from her journey of finding peace, power, joy, love, and light in the midst of trauma, sadness and awakening. When not writing you'll find her studying for a doctoral degree, creating in her Goddess Café, or singing karaoke.

Hillary Beth Koenig has been a freelance editor and writer for over a decade, beginning with editing DEVOTIONALs for a Christian teen girls' website. As the wife of a service member, and mother of two, she is always finding new opportunities to build community and connect with others. Supporting small businesses, nonprofit organizations, and individuals in their written endeavors is a great honor for her.

Metris Batts-Coley is Principal Consultant of The Affiliates, LLC where she coordinates training and workshops for grant writing and volunteer management and consults in the development of nonprofit and for-profit businesses. In her capacity she also serves as a community organizer coordinating cooperative efforts and campaigning to promote the interests of her clients. A woman of faith, she takes joy in posting morning prayers encouraging social media followers.

Britany A. Brooks is a daughter, sister, aunt, friend, and aspiring author who loves the Lord dearly. She is the founder of Godly Women Circle; where women unite and strengthen each other in Christ. She's lives in Kingston, Jamaica where she works in a lead administrative role, at one of the country's most reputable companies. Britany is very enthusiastic about encouraging others to heal from a broken past; and this fuels her desire to further her studies in psychology. She urges individuals to standardize the following: If hurt people can hurt people then healed people can influence others to heal.

Evangelist Annette L. Anderson is a Motivational Speaker, Author and Quote-ologist who is passionate about storytelling, and writing poems, and inspirational messages. She is the author of two books: *Walking It Out* and *Living Life One Quote at A Time*.

She believes that if you change your mind set you will be able change your life. She is the founder of Annette L. Anderson Ministries, devoted to preaching and teaching The Word of God. She believes that it's important that we all learn to SOAR - Speak! Orate! Articulate! Reverberate!

Anita Faye Wilson has always been known for two areas of passion in her life - Ministry and Music. She spent most of her young years sharing the stage with many music industry greats including Gloria Estefan. Later she started working behind the scenes as a vocal coach, artist developer and music industry consulting. Wilson was called into the ministry in 1995. Wilson was a 2019 honoree for the United Nations Association of Broward County where she was awarded the Cultural Educator Award. She is Founder of Movement Worldwide Inc. and Eat Well Live Well Be Well LLC.

E Claudette Freeman is an award-winning playwright, novelist, award-winning radio journalist and Publisher and Lead Editor of Pecan Tree Publishing and its imprints. Freeman is the author of three books, two series of journals, a dozen plays and is a sought-after commissioned playwright. When not writing, she loves watching old TV shows, Dateline, and 48 Hours, and sitting in South Florida parks watching iguanas and squirrels do their things. She is the proud mother of one son, Isaiah, and a doggy-grandma to Dolce.